LEADERS LIFT

Steve Hagen

www.NeverFlinch.com

A HUGE THANK YOU TO AMY, NASH, HANNA, WIL, AND SOREN! YOU'VE INSPIRED ME TO BECOME THE BEST LEADER THAT I CAN BECOME.

THANK YOU TO JOEL, ANDY AND DOC! WITHOUT YOUR FORESIGHT AND INSIGHT, THIS BOOK WOULD HAVE NOT BEEN POSSIBLE.

AND LAST BUT CERTAINLY NOT LEAST, THANK YOU TO COACH LOU HOLTZ, BUTCH DAVIS, CHRIS AULT, AND ALL THE OTHER MANY COACHES THAT I'VE COACHED WITH AND ALONGSIDE.

IT'S A GREAT RIDE!!!

Similar to Lessons from the Locker Room, these too are a bunch of different notes, lessons, and stories that I've picked up along the way. I wrote these down in my own personal notes that I've taken in staff meetings, clinics, or have just learned through trial and error. I didn't learn everything about leadership all at once. I started playing sports when I was a little guy, and started coaching when I was 22 years old.

I know I've changed, but I don't think the time tested basic leadership principles have changed much at all. It's like asking did the Bible change, or did reading the Bible change me? Realizing you're the leader will change you.

I've been fortunate to have coached on many different football staffs and under many different styles of leaders, some lead by example, some by fear and force, others lead by less forceful methods; Nevertheless, all methods were about teaching and demanding the best out of every player. All of them were designed to test the individual and prove to him that the team is stronger than the individual.

You may not think you're a leader, but if your someone's Mom, Dad, Brother, Sister, Aunt, Uncle, Friend, Teacher, Pastor, Team Mate (you get the idea), someone most likely is looking at you. So with that being said, be a positive, inspiring, motivating, encouraging leader that brings out the very best in everyone!

I've coached a lot of football throughout my career, and learned from a bunch of different leaders. I've been an assistant, I've been a coordinator, and I've been a Head Coach. I've worked with some great leaders, listened to others, and I have read from many. I've coached from Pop Warner to Pro football, and leadership is all about the same on every level, minus a few dollars here and there. In my mind, it comes down to this:

The leader establishes the direction and creates a feeling of ownership and accountability in the "Team." He must influence, inspire, and motivate the individuals to work together as one team to achieve a common goal that they can totally and completely own, and in the end have pride in their performance.

Sometimes while editing this book I thought it seemed a bit out of order, but then I thought about how I learned all this stuff. I didn't learn all this information in one class, in one day or even in one year. It's been a lifetime of learning that has been taught to me by many teachers throughout my life. There were times that I wrote something down three years previous that hit me differently today. I'm sure I'll read this in another three years, and it'll take on even more meaning. Each day I learn, grow, share, and learn some more. That's what it's all about. Leadership is a form of art, everyone does it differently.

I know this, good **Leaders Lift**!!! They Lift Spirits, they Lift People, and they Lift Life!!!

ENJOY THE JOURNEY!!!

LIFE'S LESSONS ARE LEARNED IN BITS AND PIECES OVER TIME. AND LIKE A PUZZLE THAT SLOWLY COMES TOGETHER, WE EVENTUALLY BECOME WHO WE ARE!

— AMY GRANT —

There is no greater job on the planet than to be someone's parent. Amy and I are the parents of four children, and it's our honor to lead them. Fortunately I was blessed to have loving parents who guided my steps. As Cleeve McCleary would say, "I had a serious drug problem."

"My parents drug me to school,
They drug me to practice

and

They drug me church every Sunday!"

My dad never got a college education, but he made sure all his kids had the opportunity to get one. My parents understood hard work and discipline. My dad is a World War II veteran, and I'm proud of him! My mom taught school, and actually taught me in the second grade, no getting out of homework for me. Most importantly, they set me up to be intelligent, confident, and successful! Like Coach Holtz would say, "I've been 18 son, you've never been 42!" My parents got that! They had great foresight and weren't afraid to use it.

My dad got me my first job when I was 8 years old, as a ball boy for the Dallas Cowboys, and ever since that day it's been the cornerstone of my career. When the Equipment Manager for the Cowboys asked him if he knew of anyone that had any boys that would like to be ball boys he said, "Yes sir, I've got four of my own!" The rest is history. Every job that I've ever had from that day has been connected to that very first one. Hard work, honesty, discipline, integrity, commitment, you tell me when it's too early to start learning those qualities.

Thanks Mom and Dad, you LIFTED ME
and showed me how to LIFT MINE!!!

I haven't worked in any other business other than football. I have a good feel for what it takes to be successful as a leader on a team sport. I think that this experience can relate to a lot of other "business teams" too. There are many forms of "teams", not all are sports related, but all teams need leadership! A few things that the leader must get across to the team is that the

1. TEAM COMES FIRST,
2. It's not MY TEAM, but OUR TEAM,
3. and everyone on the team is CONNECTED ALL THE TIME.!

The TEAM COMES FIRST is the most important thought process of any team. We say it in my own family, OUR FAMILY COMES FIRST! It's not about one player or one family member, it's about all of US, not just ME. It's a WE Thing!!!

Here's another thought:

4. LEADERS ARE USELESS without FOLLOWERS

Don't forget who we're here to serve! Parents aren't parents, unless they have children. In school we don't have students because we have a faculty, we have a faculty because we have students, we have drill sargents because we have soldiers, coaches because we have players. Players can still play, but coaches can't coach. Leaders are there to serve and assist.

I was driving home from my 10 year old, Wil's, basketball practice the other night, and he asked me, "Daddy, who coaches the 30 year old guys in the Rec League?" I told him, "They probably don't have a coach, they probably coach themselves."

Not all Players need Coaches, but all Coaches need Players!

Manny Pacquiao's trainer, Freddie Roach, said it like this in the USA Today,

"I think I have the best fighters in the world, that's why I'm the best trainer when the bell rings, I sit down and they fight. My key to success is hanging out with great fighters."

There's a little more to it than that, but there's a lot of truth to that statement.

WHY DO GUYS FOLLOW?

Because they believe! They believe they're going to become something more than they already are. They believe they're going to be part of something bigger than themselves!

I've realized that any act of generosity, large or small, truly makes a difference. It becomes a strand of hope woven permanently into the fabric of life. When you give something, you become a part of something bigger than yourself.

— Amy Grant —

Football coaches design Spring Football practice for a lot of reasons:

* One is to find out who they have for next season,
* Another is to develop their talent base
* And still another is to "weed out" the ones that can't handle what the season will bring

All in all, it's designed to bring out the best in the players and the team.

BOOT CAMP IN THE MILITARY AND SPRING FOOTBALL HAVE SOME SIMILARITIES. IT IS A TIME TO FIND OUT WHO CAN HANDLE WHAT'S ABOUT TO HAPPEN!!! BOOT CAMP IS A "SCREENING OUT PROCESS. THEY TRY TO MAKE THE QUITTERS QUIT. SOME OF IT IS DONE THROUGH FEAR, BUT MOST OF IT IS ABOUT REALITY! THE REALITY OF WHAT'S GOING TO HAPPEN. ARE YOU GOING TO BE ABLE TO HANDLE WHAT'S ABOUT TO HAPPEN? IF THEY'RE GOING TO QUIT, IT'S BEST TO FIND OUT EARLIER RATHER THAN LATER. LET'S NOT FIND OUT WHEN IT GETS DOWN TO CRUNCH TIME THAT THIS GUYS GOING TO QUIT, LET'S FIND OUT NOW. IT'S A TIME WHERE THE LEADER TAKES A BUNCH OF INDIVIDUALS AND MAKES THEM HOLD EACH OTHER AND THEMSELVES ACCOUNTABLE TO THE TEAM AND ONE ANOTHER. SOME MEN CAN'T HANDLE IT, MOST MEN CAN, BUT DON'T KNOW IT!!!

SPRING FOOTBALL AND TWO-A-DAYS ARE ALL ABOUT FINDING OUT WHO CAN PLAY AND WHERE THEY CAN PLAY. THIS WEEDING OUT PROCESS IS WHAT HELPS THE INDIVIDUAL PLAYERS AND THE TEAM GET STRONGER. PLAYERS DEFINE THEIR ROLES, VERY RARELY DO THE COACHES HAVE TO SET THE DEPTH CHART, THE PLAYERS DO IT THEMSELVES BY WHO THEY ARE AND HOW THEY COMPETE.

AFTER THE QUITTERS ARE GONE AND THOSE WHO HAVE SURVIVED THE TESTS, PHYSICAL AND MENTAL REMAIN, THEN YOU HAVE THE BEGINNING INGREDIENTS OF A TEAM. WINNERS AND LOSERS AREN'T BORN, THEY'RE TRAINED. MOTHERS DON'T GIVE BIRTH TO DR.'S

LAWYERS, SCIENTISTS, MUSICIANS OR NATIONAL CHAMPIONS.
THEY GIVE BIRTH TO SONS AND DAUGHTERS WHO BECOME...
CHAMPIONS!

SO NOW WE GET TO THIS:

WHY DO GUYS FOLLOW?

1. BECAUSE THEY BELIEVE IN THE DIRECTION.
2. THEY ARE MOTIVATED, INSPIRED AND ENCOURAGED TO FOLLOW.

ENCOURAGE — TO PUT COURAGE INTO, THE LEADER ENCOURAGES ACTION, HE PUTS COURAGE INTO THE PLAYERS

3. THEY WANT TO OWN THEIR ACTIONS!

AND

4. THEY WANT TO BE PART OF SOMETHING GREAT!

YOU KNOW
"THOSE WHO STAY WILL BECOME CHAMPIONS!!!"

JESUS SAID IT BEST

"FOLLOW ME

AND I WILL MAKE YOU FISHERS OF MEN!"

MARK 1:17

THE WORDS I WILL ARE HUGE! JESUS DIDN'T SAY, HEY TRY THIS AND MAYBE YOU WILL MAKE SOMETHING OF YOUR LIFE.

HE SAID FOLLOW ME AND I WILL MAKE SOMETHING OUT OF YOU AND HE DOES!!!

HE GAVE THOSE FIRST DISCIPLES DIRECTION, INSPIRED AND ENCOURAGED THEM. THEY KNEW THEY WERE GOING TO BE PART OF SOMETHING GREAT!

– HOW TO LEAD –

＊ THERE'S LEADING BY EXAMPLE.

＊ THERE'S LEADING BY EXPERIENCE, FORESIGHT AND THOUGHTFULNESS.

＊ THERE'S LEADING BY FEAR

(FEAR IS A FORM OF LEADERSHIP DESIGNED TO GET RID OF THE FEARFUL.
WHEN USED OVER A LONG TERM IT CAN BREED RESENTMENT AND MAL-
CONTENT. WHAT MOTIVATES ONE MAY DESTROY ANOTHER)

＊ GOOD LEADERSHIP IS INTANGIBLE UNTIL IT SHOWS UP IN PERFORMANCE!!!

LEADERS SHOULD DEVELOP MORE LEADERS,
NOT JUST MORE FOLLOWERS.

THAT MAY SOUND CRAZY AFTER HAVING SAID WHAT I JUST SAID,
LEADERS ARE USELESS WITHOUT FOLLOWERS, BUT THIS IS ABOUT TURNING
THE FOLLOWER INTO A LEADER. TO FOLLOW IS TO LET SOMEONE ELSE
TAKE OWNERSHIP, TO LET SOMEONE ELSE BE ACCOUNTABLE AND RE-
SPONSIBLE. TO LEAD IS TO OWN IT!!!

I HEARD A MARINE SAY THIS ONE TIME:

MEN DON'T FAIL, IT'S THE LEADER THAT FAILS THEM!
THEY FAIL TO BRING THE MEN UP TO
ACHIEVE THEIR BEST!!!

AS LEADERS, OUR ATTITUDE HAS A POWERFUL IMPACT ON OTH-
ERS. POSITIVE OR NEGATIVE, IT'S ALL BASED ON OUR ATTITUDE. WE, AS
LEADERS HAVE AN OBLIGATION TO DEVELOP A POSITIVE ATTITUDE THAT IN-
SPIRES PEOPLE TO BECOME MORE THAN THEY EVER THOUGHT THEY COULD
BE, SET HIGH STANDARDS, AND MOTIVATE THEM TO ACHIEVE THEIR DREAMS.

TONY DUNGY SAID THIS TO HIS TEAMS
NO EXCUSES, NO EXPLANATIONS!

WHEN I WAS AT NOTRE DAME WITH COACH HOLTZ WE HAD A SIGN UP IN OUR LOCKER ROOM THAT READ:

WINNING IS NEVER ACCIDENTAL!

YOU GET WHAT YOU EMPHASIZE!

I HAVE ALWAYS LOVED OUR FIRST MEETING AT NOTRE DAME WHEN COACH HOLTZ WOULD ADDRESS THE FRESHMAN. THE MEETING WOULD GO SOMETHING LIKE THIS. SIT UP AND LISTEN UP MEN! EVERYONE OF YOU IS FROM SOMEWHERE DIFFERENT, SOME FROM TEXAS, SOME FROM CALIFORNIA, SOME FROM GEORGIA, AND SOME FROM THE MID-WEST, I CAN ASSURE EVERYONE IN THIS ROOM THAT WE ARE NOT GOING TO BECOME YOU. YOU MUST BECOME NOTRE DAME. I WANT YOU TO LEARN EVERYTHING WE DO AT NOTRE DAME, WHEN WE DO IT, HOW WE DO IT, AND WHY WE DO IT. IT'S IMPORTANT THAT YOU LEARN OUR METHODS NOW, SO THAT WHEN YOU BECOME JUNIORS AND SENIORS YOU CAN PROVIDE THE PROPER LEADERSHIP FOR OUR YOUNGER PLAYERS. WE DID NOT RECRUIT YOU TO CHANGE NOTRE DAME, BUT TO CONFORM TO THE MORALS AND VALUES OF THIS GREAT UNIVERSITY. YOU WON'T CHANGE NOTRE DAME, BUT NOTRE DAME IS GOING TO CHANGE YOU!!!

WE HAVE A STANDARD AND DEMAND EXCELLENCE. NOW IT'S UP TO YOU!!!

FUNDAMENTALS WIN!!

A single man walks into a pet store looking to buy a pet. He looks at the birds and notices they all cost $2.50, except one, which was $595! He asked the store owner, "How come this one is so expensive? He looks identical to the others". "Ah that's where you're wrong" replied the owner, "This one can talk and sing! Those other birds just sit there." The man thought about it for a minute and decided that this bird might be good company, so he bought it. The next day he returned to the store angry and in search of the owner He said, "I paid $595 for that bird and it doesn't talk or sing!" The owner asked, "What did the bird do after he rang his bell?" The man said "What bell?" "The bell he rings to tune himself." The owner said. "If he can't tune himself he can't talk or sing I've got a bell here for $21." So the guy bought the bell.

He returned the next day more irate than ever He complained to the owner, "My bird rang the bell, and he still hasn't said one word." "That's impossible," said the owner, "I have the same bird, and just this morning he woke up, rang his little bell, blew his whistle and talked my head off." The man stopped him and said, "What whistle?" The owner said, "You mean to tell me you didn't buy the whistle? That bird won't sing until he blows his whistle. I have a whistle on sale today for $19." The guy bought the whistle. Over the next three days the man went back and bought a ladder, a bird bath, and a swing At the end of the week the customer returned to the store in tears and told the owner that his bird finally talked. He told him, his bird woke up early, rang his bell blew his whistle, climbed his ladder, swung on his swing and keeled over in his bath. Just before he died, he looked over at me and said, "Couldn't you buy any bird seed?"

IT'S NOT ALL ABOUT THE BELLS AND WHISTLES,

FUNDAMENTALS WIN!!!

LESS IS MORE

ONE OF THE ONLY THINGS WE HAVE IN COMMON IS TIME. WE ALL ONLY HAVE 24 HOURS IN OUR DAY. HOW WE USE THOSE HOURS DEFINES US.

IN FOOTBALL LESS WORDS USED TO CALL A PLAY

EQUALS

LESS TIME TO CALL A PLAY

EQUALS

MORE PLAYS CALLED IN A GAME.

EQUALS

MORE OPPORTUNITIES TO SCORE!!!

LESS PLAYS TO EXECUTE TO PERFECTION

EQUALS

LESS MISTAKES MADE IN A GAME

EQUALS

MORE PERFECTLY EXECUTED PLAYS

EQUALS

MORE OPPORTUNITIES TO SCORE POINTS.

EQUALS

MORE VICTORIES!!!

I'VE ALWAYS THOUGHT IT WAS CRAZY TO HAVE A 1000 DIFFERENT PLAYS IN OUR PLAYBOOK THAT WE CAN ONLY PRACTICE ONE TIME A WEEK. WE NEED GOOD REPS!

I THINK GOD GAVE MOSES ONLY TEN COMMANDMENTS TO BRING DOWN TO THE PEOPLE BECAUSE HE KNEW THAT WAS ALL THEY COULD HANDLE. AND WE'VE PROVED THAT WE CAN'T EVEN HANDLE THOSE TEN. MAYBE THAT'S WHY GOD TRIED AGAIN IN THE NEW TESTAMENT WITH JESUS JUST TELLING US THE GREATEST COMMANDMENT OF ALL: LOVE YOUR NEIGHBOR AS YOURSELF. GOD TOOK IT FROM TEN TO ONE. JUST TRYING TO KEEP IT SIMPLE!

10 → 1

I heard Tony Dungy of the Colts say this in an interview one time when their defense was struggling
"We don't need to add one more defense, we need to understand and play the ones we have better!"

KEEPING IT SIMPLE

I coached about nine 5 and 6 year olds to play football one season. I taught them 3 offensive plays, that was it, just three, and we won all our games! This is how simple it was:

Play #1 — Run Right was what we called "Cowboy"
Play #2 — Fake Run Right Reverse we called "Rodeo"
Play #3 — Fake Run Right Pass we called "Slingshot"!

Really simple, fun, and easy for the kids to identify with, I told them one word and they knew how to line up, where to line up, and what to do. Eventually, we got good and they were telling me to run Rodeo or Slingshot, that's when I knew we were good. They owned it and had a blast with it. All the plays looked similar to their opponent, but weren't. We made the same plays look different, and different plays look the same.

Every kid on the team knew those plays, that's all the plays that we practiced, we spent the rest of our time practicing blocking, catching, running, and pulling flags. We invested our time into practicing the Fundamentals, coaching the players, and emphasized raising their level of confidence. The kids knew that we played faster and got more plays called with a lot less mistakes, which gave our team more opportunities to score, which gave us a

BETTER CHANCE TO WIN. HOW'D THEY KNOW THAT? BECAUSE I TOLD THEM THAT'S WHO THEY WERE. I TOLD THEM THEY'RE SMART, FAST, AND GREAT! WE CREATED A VISION FOR THEM, AND MADE THEM LIVE UP TO, AND EXCEL AT THEIR IDENTITY. WE DID ONE THING 1000 TIMES, AND DID IT BETTER EVERY DAY!

LEARNED BEHAVIOR BECOMES REACTIONS,
REACTIONS BECOME INSTINCTS.
LET'S GET SOME REPS!!!

WOODY HAYES SAID IT LIKE THIS —

"YOU CAN SAY ONE THING 1000 TIMES OR 1000 THINGS ONE TIME. YOU TELL ME WHAT'S BEST!"

IT CAN BE THAT SIMPLE! LEADING PEOPLE IS NOT TRIPLE TRIGONOMETRY. IT SHOULD BE SIMPLE, CREATIVE, AND FUN! PEOPLE NEED TO FEEL LIKE THEY HAVE A CHANCE TO WIN. A PLAYER WILL FOLLOW THE COACH OR PLAYER WHO GIVES HIM THE MOST CONFIDENCE. WE, AS LEADERS / COACHES / TEACHERS / PARENTS, HAVE TO CREATE A POSITIVE ENVIRONMENT. LEADERS HAVE THE ULTIMATE RESPONSIBILITY OF TRAINING THEIR PEOPLE, BECAUSE EVERY JOB REQUIRES TRAINING!

COACH SAM RATTIGLIANO,
FORMER CLEVELAND BROWNS HEAD COACH TOLD ME THIS ONE TIME

" ENCOURAGEMENT IS THE OXYGEN TO OUR SOULS"

I LOVE THAT!!!

A LEADER MUST ENCOURAGE OTHERS TO STRUGGLE, AND ASSURE THEM THAT THE STRUGGLES ARE WORTHWHILE AND VALUABLE!

"WE ARE IN THE MOST POWERFUL PROFESSION
ON THE PLANET"

COACH TOM OSBORNE WAS TALKING TO THE NATIONAL
FOOTBALL COACHES ASSOCIATION. HE WAS REFERRING TO HAVING THE
ABILITY TO REACH OUT, INFLUENCE, AND ENCOURAGE YOUNG MEN IN
A POWERFULLY PRODUCTIVE WAY, USING THE GAME OF FOOTBALL AS
OUR TOOL.

FLORIDA GATOR'S TEAM ROOM

TALENT WILL GET US
7 - 8 WINS
TALENT + LEADERSHIP WILL GET US
9 - 10 WINS
TALENT + LEADERSHIP + OWNERSHIP
WILL GET US A
CHAMPIONSHIP

"WE ARE NOT GOING TO WIN BECAUSE YOU HAVE A NEW HEAD
COACH, ANYMORE THAN YOU ARE GOING TO FIX A FLAT TIRE BY
CHANGING THE DRIVER. WE WILL WIN THE SECOND ALL OF US
GET RID OF OUR LAME EXCUSES,
CHANGE OUR ATTITUDES, AND BUY IN!"
— BUTCH DAVIS —

Peter Ueberroth,
    former MLB Commissioner
    "We can accomplish anything when enough people care."

——————————//——————————

Every successful coach that I've ever worked with always had a plan and worked the plan. I've also worked with some others who didn't have a plan and flew by the seat of their pants.

"Failure to prepare is preparing to fail!"
                    Joe Paterno

Coach Holtz's plan at Notre Dame was simple:
※ ATTITUDE — It all starts with ATTITUDE!
    — Your TALENT determines what you can do!
    — Your MOTIVATION determines how much you're willing to do!
                    and
    — Your ATTITUDE determines how well you do it!

Trappist monks are renowned for their amazing vows of silence. It's incredible the amount of self restraint these monks display. This certain Monk was only allowed to say two words every year. After the first year he met with his Superior Brother and said, "Bad Bed!"
After the second year he came back to say, "Bad Food!"
After the third year of silence he came back to say, "No TV!" Another silent year passed, and this time when he met with his Brother Superior he handed him his robes and sandals and announced "I Quit!" Brother Superior replied, "Well don't expect me to try to dissuade you. You've done nothing but complain since you got here."

ATTITUDE!!!

Negative thinking will produce exactly what it promises —
NOTHING!

✳ <u>ADVERSITY</u> — expect it, deal with it, and overcome it!
Get your attitude right!

Coach Osborne said it like this:
"When facing Adversity, some teams quit, some teams blame others, and some teams Learn! We choose to Learn!"

God often doesn't give you what you need until you've stuck your feet in the water. It was when Moses put his feet in the water, and Pharaoh's army was coming down to capture and kill him, that the Red Sea parted and Moses and the people of Israel walked across to freedom!

✳ <u>SENSE OF PURPOSE</u> — What's your role on the team? What's our mission as a team.

The greater danger for most of us lies not in setting our aim too high and falling short; but in setting our aim too low and achieving our mark.
— Michelangelo —

History is always shaped
by one person with a vision!

✳ <u>SACRIFICE</u> — Take pride in sacrifice! Why is sacrifice so vital to any game plan? The answer is simple. So few people are willing to make them. Winners Sacrifice!!!

1/96TH

I HAVE THE FRACTION 1/96TH WRITTEN ON MY BOARD IN BIG BLACK, BOLD INK, IN THE FRONT OF MY TIGHT END ROOM. WHENEVER MY GUYS GET A LITTLE SALTY, OR SIDETRACKED, OR MAYBE THEY THINK THEY'RE WORKING TOO HARD AND START TO COMPLAIN, I TELL THEM TO TAKE A LOOK UP AT THE BOARD, AND REMIND THEM THAT, "WE COULD ALL BE FLIPPIN' BURGERS FOR A LIVING" IT KIND OF BRINGS IT ALL BACK INTO PERSPECTIVE. WE ARE ONE OF THE NINETY SIX TIGHT ENDS THAT ARE GETTING PAID TO PLAY FOOTBALL IN THE NFL. THE SACRIFICES YOU MAKE KEEPS YOU IN YOUR POSITION. WHAT ARE YOU 1/96TH OF?

✳ ADAPTABILITY –

SCOREBOARD

WHY IS THERE A SCOREBOARD IN EVERY GAME? THERE'S A SCOREBOARD BECAUSE IT SHOWS YOU EXACTLY WHERE YOU ARE AT THAT EXACT MOMENT IN THE GAME. IT TELLS YOU WHAT NEEDS TO BE DONE AND WHERE YOU NEED TO GO. IT SHOWS EVERYONE THAT LOOKS AT IT WHAT NEEDS TO CHANGE. IT ALLOWS THE TEAMS TO ADAPT TO THE TIME AND SITUATION OF THAT PARTICULAR MOMENT OF THE GAME..

EVERY COACH, PLAYER AND FAN UNDERSTANDS THE SCOREBOARD. A FAN CAN COME INTO A GAME 15 MINUTES LATE AND GET A PRETTY GOOD FEEL FOR THE GAME JUST BY CHECKING OUT THE SCOREBOARD.

EVERY LEADER NEEDS A SCOREBOARD, WHETHER IT'S A BUDGET, OR A BALANCE SHEET, ANY KIND OF INDICATOR THAT TELLS YOU WHERE YOU ARE AND WHERE THE TEAM IS HEADING. HOW CAN YOU TELL WHO WINS IF YOU DON'T KEEP SCORE? HOW DO YOU KNOW HOW MUCH TIME YOU HAVE LEFT WITHOUT A SCOREBOARD? IF YOU JUST WANT TO GO FOR A LITTLE DRIVE THROUGH THE COUNTRY SIDE WITH SOME BUDDIES, THEN YOU DON'T NEED SCOREBOARD. BUT IF YOU'RE TRYING TO WIN DAYTONA, THEN YOU AND YOUR TEAM BETTER KNOW HOW YOU'RE DOING!!! YOU NEED A SCOREBOARD!!!

COACH HOLTZ USED TO SAY THIS, IT REMINDED US OF THE
SCOREBOARD.

> I AM NOT WHAT I OUGHT TO BE,
> I AM NOT WHAT I'M GOING TO BE,
> BUT THANK GOD, I'M NOT WHAT I USED TO BE!

DREAM BIG — DREAMS ARE THE FUEL FOR ENTHUSIASM! DREAMERS MOVE THE WORLD!

I REMEMBER WHEN I WOULD BRING A RECRUIT INTO COACH HOLTZ'S OFFICE AT NOTRE DAME. HE WOULD HAVE THEM SIT DOWN WITH HIS FAMILY AND AFTER ASKING THEM IF THEY HAD A NICE VISIT, HE'D CUT TO THE CHASE. HE WANTED AND NEEDED TO KNOW IF THEY WERE GOING TO COMMIT TO ACCEPTING A SCHOLARSHIP. HE WOULD TALK TO THEM ABOUT THEIR DREAMS AND GOALS. AFTER LISTENING TO THEM HE WOULD TELL THEM THAT CHOOSING NOTRE DAME WAS NOT A FOUR YEAR DECISION, BUT MORE LIKE A FORTY YEAR DECISION. REALISTICALLY, IT'S A LIFETIME DECISION. COACH WOULD PULL OUT HIS BOTTOM DRAWER OF HIS FILING CABINET AND SHOW THE FAMILY ALL THE FILES OF NOTRE DAME ALUMNI THAT WERE WILLING TO HELP. HE WOULD TALK TO THEM ABOUT DREAMING BIG DREAMS, AND TELL THEM, "NOW'S YOUR CHANCE. MOST KIDS CAN ONLY DREAM OF PLAYING HERE, ONLY A FEW CAN ACHIEVE IT." THAT'S PRETTY MUCH ALL IT TOOK. HE FORECASTED A VISION FOR THE FAMILY AND LEAD THEM ON THE PATH TO ACHIEVE GOALS THAT THEY DREAMED ABOUT. DREAM BIG!!!

TOUGH — "EVERYONE HAS A PLAN UNTIL THEY ARE HIT"
— EVANDER HOLYFIELD —

BOXING FOOTBALL, HOCKEY OR JUST LIFE, EVERYONE HAS A PLAN UNTIL THEY GET HIT. "TOUGH TIMES NEVER LAST, TOUGH PEOPLE DO"!

<u>TRUST</u> – "Every relationship is based on trust! Any dishonest player will be <u>DROPPED</u> from the team. <u>DROPPED</u> means <u>DROPPED</u>, because we will not tolerate dishonesty!"

Bo Shembechler

<u>COMMITMENT</u> – <u>My Bad</u> – <u>My Bench!</u>

How "the Bench" can motivate players is amazing! Some parents use it at home, it's called, "Time Out"! Any player worth his salt doesn't like "The Bench." I was coaching a team that had a bad habit of saying "My Bad!" A guy would drop a pass, "My Bad," a QB would make the wrong read, "My Bad," a lineman would miss his block, "My Bad." It was too easy to say "My Bad." They thought if they said "My Bad," it got them off the hook, or that it was OK and that they were taking responsibility for their action. They thought it kind of protected them from the ramifications. It almost became a disease, so we had to put a stop to it. If it was "your bad" then you owned it and you had to change it. We turned "My Bad" into "My Bench"! If you said "My Bad", we said "My Bench", and they sat out! We added a little more sense of urgency and responsibility to their "My Bad" game. We told them, "if you want to change your team, then change yourself first." Amazingly, everyone got "My Bad," "My Bench" real quick!!!

"You ask me how important our weight room conditioning program is, I'll explain it like this: The weight room and church are not too different. Some kids want to be 400 lb. bench pressers but aren't real dedicated to what goes on in our weight room. That's like only going to church on Christmas and Easter, it doesn't work that way!

– Tom Osborne –

<u>TEAM FIRST</u> – FIRST WE'LL BE BEST! THEN WILL BE FIRST!
BOBBY BOWDEN FROM FLORIDA STATE ONCE SAID THIS WHEN HE WAS
ACCUSED OF RUNNING UP THE SCORE:
"IT'S NOT MY JOB TO KEEP THE SCORE DOWN. I CAN ONLY COACH
ONE TEAM, THAT'S MINE. I CAN'T COACH YOURS AND MINE. IF YOU
DON'T WANT TO GET BEAT BADLY, GET BETTER ATHLETES, COACH BETTER,
OR CHANGE YOUR SCHEDULE."
COACH HOLTZ USE TO SAY 90% OF THE PEOPLE YOU MEET DON'T
CARE ABOUT YOUR TROUBLES AND THE OTHER 10% ARE GLAD YOU HAVE
THEM. TAKE CARE OF YOUR OWN TEAM AND ONLY YOUR TEAM.

IT'S NOT JUST WANTING TO DO THE RIGHT THING IT'S KNOWING HOW TO
DO IT!!!

HARD WORK BEATS TALENT
WHEN TALENT DOESN'T WORK HARD!
HANGING IN OKLAHOMA'S WEIGHT ROOM

SIGNS THAT YOUR LEADERSHIP SKILLS
NEED SOME POLISHING
<u>YOU'RE INACCESSIBLE</u>

YOUR PEOPLE CAN'T FIND YOU, GET TO YOU, OR WHEN THEY DO, YOU
DON'T LISTEN. YOU'RE SOMEWHERE ELSE EVEN WHEN YOU'RE THERE.
DON'T BE ALOOF.

INTERACTION FUELS ACTION!

Everything rises and falls on leadership. Before there is leadership, there is communication. You must be able to communicate to lead others effectively! There are instruments in leadership, just like in a band. A band without a drum is like leadership without communication.

You're Threatening

Do you use threats? Have you ever been on the other end of those threats? That's not the greatest feeling in the world. Sometimes reality is a big enough threat in itself. There are other ways to teach and communicate, that are far more effective, and last a lot longer without the resentment.

Have you ever heard of "catch 'em doing something right." Sometimes we as leaders are so quick to point out the negatives. "Catch 'em doing something right" and let them and everybody else know what a great job they did. Think about what motivates us to do more and to do better? A good sense of well being is a great place to start! Don't put 'em down, when you can Put 'em up!

Bo Schembechler of Michigan said it best:

"You're not going to yell your way to the top of your profession. If your people are going to perform their absolute best, you need to give them the tools to do so."

You lack common courtesy and respect

"It's right out of Coaching 101. If you tell players they're not good enough all week long, they probably won't be good enough in the game."
— Bob Ladouceur —

YOUR TEAM'S MORALE IS LOW?

Why is the morale low? The morale is low because of poor accessibility to the leader, poor communication from the leader, and threatening tactics directed from the leader that degrades and demoralizes the spirit of the team. I think good or bad morale is a by-product of all the relationships, or lack of relationships in and among the team. Just like winning is a by-product of good healthy team relationships, so is morale. What comes first, winning or good morale? The chicken or the egg? I'm not sure but I do know this, it's hard to have one without the other.

THE TEAM IS SECOND TO INDIVIDUAL PERKS.

I once worked on a football staff that was rewarded like this, whoever signed the most recruits on signing day won a big colored TV. Now at first thought you might think that's not all bad, but think about that for a minute. Is it the coach who signs the most players? Or is it the coach who signs the best players? Ask Gideon that question. (Judges 7:7)

A coach may not have as many players in his area, but he may have the best player in his area. Should we as a staff all work together to get that best player or should we work as individuals to get the most players? I'll give you a hint. The most players don't always win games, but more often than not the best players do.

You may not always win with good players, but you definitely won't win without them!
CHRIS AULT

NICE MOVIE! THE ULTIMATE GIFT

I've always liked the movie "The Ultimate Gift". It's a story about a billionaire named Red Stevens and his extended family. In the movie he has passed, but left a few "Inheritance Gifts" for his family. One of the greatest gifts is the one he left for his estranged grandson, Jason. All Red's children, including Jason, had been spoiled by Red's riches. A life of extreme privilege and an absent father had molded selfish and uncaring children. Red knew this and wanted it rectified. In so doing he left a series of video tapes for Jason to watch and learn from before he could receive his gift. Initially, Jason was an ingrate, he didn't get it, and acted like his mother and uncles. As he embarked on his grandfather's journey, the puzzle started to reveal itself.

Here are the gifts that Jason inherited from his grandfather Red —

THE GIFT OF WORK — Work for what you earn, you might appreciate it more! Proverbs 6:6-11

THE GIFT OF FRIENDS — Gen 2:18 Everyone needs a friend! We're all connected! John 15:12

THE GIFT OF MONEY — Money's good, so is sharing it! Proverbs 19:17

THE GIFT OF GRATITUDE — Be grateful for every gift, great or small! Eph. 2:8

THE GIFT OF A DAY — Every day has it's own value! Matthew 6:25

THE GIFT OF DREAMS — Everything's possible! Mark 9:23, 1 John 5:14-15

The "ULTIMATE GIFT" is what we learn and who we become. Just like leaders should develop Leaders, God Develops us to do his work. He is the Ultimate leader, developing more leaders to do his work. That's what Leaders do, It's all part of the Grand Plan!

1. LEADERS ARE THOUGHTFUL
WHAT CAN I DO TODAY TO BRING OUT THE BEST IN MY TEAM?

2. LEADERS COOPERATE!!!
WE'RE ALL CONNECTED ALL THE TIME!

3. LEADERS ARE HONEST!!!
IF THE TRUTH KILLS A MAN, LET HIM DIE!
— HARRY TRUMAN —

THERE ARE NO VERSIONS OF THE TRUTH!
— SOMETHING'S GOT TO GIVE —

4. LEADERS HANDLE PRESSURE!!!
PRESSURE HAPPENS WHEN YOU ARE CALLED UPON AND YOU ARE NOT PREPARED TO HANDLE THE TASK.
TONY LA RUSSA

5. LEADERS ARE GRATEFUL
HAVE AN ATTITUDE OF GRATITUDE.
BE GRATEFUL!!

ZIG ZIGLAR

6. Leaders are Humble

Bobby Bowden Florida State's Head Football Coach put it this way:

"A HALO AND A NOOSE ARE 12 INCHES AND ONE
KNOT AWAY.

BE HUMBLE!"

LOVE IT!!!

Nelson Mandela said it best

"ONE TEAM, ONE NATION"   GOOGLE IT!

I can't even do this story justice, so to YouTube and click on Nelson Mandela espy awards.

7. Leaders Listen!

Listen while you lead –
You cannot lead if you do not listen!

– LISTEN!!! –

A lawyer asked the man, "Didn't you tell the Highway Patrolman that your were fine, after he asked you? The man replied, "Well my favorite mule Bessie..." The lawyer interrupted and shouted, "Just answer the question!" "I am," the man replied. And started again with, "my favorite mule." Again the lawyer jumped in and said, "Your Honor, he's not answering the question!" The lawyer wanted to trap him with his own words, but the Judge said, "Hold on here for a minute, I want to hear about your mule Bessie."

"Well your Honor," the man started back, "I had just put Bessie back in her trailer, and started to drive off when all of a sudden we got blind – sided by a big Semi-truck. It hit us so hard that the collision threw me from my truck

AND BESSIE FROM HER TRAILER, SHE FLEW INTO THE DITCH ON THE FAR SIDE OF THE ROAD, AND I LANDED ON THE OTHER SIDE. FROM WHERE I WAS LAYING I COULD HEAR HER MOANING. WHEN THE PATROLMAN ARRIVED AT THE SCENE AND SAW HOW BADLY BESSIE WAS INJURED, HE PULLED OUT HIS GUN AND SHOT HER BETWEEN THE EYES TO PUT HER OUT OF HER MISERY. THEN HE WALKED OVER TO ME WITH HIS GUN IN HIS HAND AND ASKED ME HOW I WAS DOING? I SAID "FINE!"

LISTEN, FOR THE WHOLE STORY!!!

8. LEADERS CREATE AN IDENTITY
WHO ARE WE AND WHAT DO WE REPRESENT?

I LOVE THIS!!! ⟶ WE LIVE IT!!!

WHEN I WAS AT FRESNO WE USED TO SAY WHAT COACH BAXTER CALLED THE "SPECIAL TEAMS CONSTITUTION," EVERYDAY BEFORE PRACTICE. OUR GUYS HAD THE "CONSTITUTION" MEMORIZED FROM TIP TO TOE, EVERYONE OF THEM. AS A FRESHMAN, FROM THE DAY YOU ARRIVED, YOU WERE GIVEN 24 HOURS TO HAVE IT MEMORIZED AND BE ABLE TO RECITE IT IN FRONT OF THE TEAM, NO EXCUSES, NO EXPLANATIONS!

IT WAS IMPORTANT TO EVERYONE. THE SENIORS LOVED PUTTING THE FRESHMAN UNDER THAT MICROSCOPE. WE SAID THOSE 12 POINTS THAT ENDED IN, "WE'VE GOT A BIG PLAY, BIG HIT REPUTATION!!!" EVERYDAY, EXCEPT GAME DAY. I THOUGHT THAT WAS ODD, EVERYDAY BUT GAME DAY. WHY NOT GAME DAY? SO BEING THE INQUISITIVE GUY THAT I AM, I ASKED JOHN, "WHY DO WE YELL OUT THE "CONSTITUTION" EVERY DAY BUT GAME DAY? HE SAID,

"THAT'S THE DAY WE LIVE IT!!!"

THIS IS WHAT IT'S ALL ABOUT

9. LEADERS LIFT!

GREAT LEADERS LIFT, THEY RAISE THE MORALE, THEY BREATHE LIFE INTO THE TEAM, THEY INJECT ENERGY AND ENTHUSIASM AND ARE THE LIVING EXAMPLE OF WHAT IS EXPECTED.
GREAT LEADERS LIFT!!!

OUR FRIENDS UP THE STREET HAVE A FRAMED FAMILY PICTURE HANGING IN THEIR KITCHEN THAT HAS A FAMILY STATEMENT ON IT THAT SAYS:

"WE ARE CHAMPIONS FOR GOD, WE ARE KIND AND FUN LOVING SMART AND PATIENT. OUR LOVE OF FAMILY ONLY COMES SECOND TO OUR LOVE OF GOD. FOR IT IS THROUGH CHRIST THAT WE GET ALL OUR STRENGTH AND COMFORT."

THE PROPER ENVIRONMENT MUST EXIST
OR NOTHING WILL GROW!
TRY GROWING A GARDEN ON A CEMENT SIDEWALK,
NOT SO FAST!

**** MY OLDEST SON GOES TO A SCHOOL NAMED ST. IGNATIUS AND THEY HAVE SHIRTS THAT THE BOYS WEAR THAT SAY:

MY ALL TIME FAVORITE!!!

→ "IGNATI<u>US</u>"

STARTS WITH "I" AND ENDS WITH "<u>US</u>"

MEN FOR OTHERS.

I LOVE THIS, THAT'S WHO THEY ARE AND WHO THEY REPRESENT.

Strong Leadership Principles

1. Know yourself and always seek to improve.
2. Be tactically sharp and technically sound.
3. Develop a sense of Responsibility and accountability within the Team.
4. Make sound and Timely Decisions.
5. Train the individuals to become part of a Team.
6. Know your Team and care about them (without the players, there is no game)
7. Make sure the job gets done right!
8. As a LEADER, you are the EXAMPLE!

He's all of this, & more

Great Coach!

Coach Lad

⭐ Bob Ladouceur is the Head Football Coach at De La Salle High School in Concord, California. It's an all boys Catholic school that was about 3 miles from my house when I lived in the East Bay. About 900 boys go to school there and their football teams are GOOD! Going into the 2008 season Coach Lad's record was 356 −25 −3, that's a 93% winning average!!!

Here's what one writer said about him:

He's a philosopher and a tactician, he's old school and new age. Nobody works his teams harder or stresses fundamentals more, but he will tell you that the key component to his success is the most basic of human emotions — Love!

His teams win in part because he doesn't emphasize winning. He knows that winning is a by-product of who they are and what they do. "Kids respect true humility and that you stand for something more than winning" he says. "They'll fight for you and your program if you stand for more than that."

He has broken the game down to it's DNA and discovered the secret to success. It's simple, but it's not easy. Blair Thomas, his longtime Assistant said, "Winning a lot of High School football games is doable, it's no big deal. What's difficult is getting people to understand there's more to life than football. That's what Coach Lad does." Coach Ladouceur has found a way to turn selfish teenagers into selfless teammates by making them step back and examine their relationships. Coach Lad is an absolute master in human relationships.

— When The Game Stands Tall —

I feel blessed to have had a chance to know Coach Ladouceur, I've been to De La Salle and have watched them practice and play games many times. I've coached guys that have played for Coach Lad and have had them play in Summer Football Camps. They play the best teams they can, because he knows it brings out the best in his team. At one time they had the longest winning streak in all of High School Football, at something like 151 games, a span of 11 years without losing a single game, WOW!!! Everyone around the Bay would refer to it as "The Streak". One day Coach Lad told me, "what amazes me about 'the Streak', it has been accomplished by teenagers, which indicates what theses kids are capable of doing".

When you talk about a guy that "Gets It"! Coach Lad not only "Gets It", he "Gives It" and that's an UNDERSTATEMENT!!!

☆ ME IS NOT WE
THERE'S A REASON WHY THE WORD
INDIVIDUAL STARTS WITH THE LETTER "I".

※ TRUST ACTIONS, NOT WORDS.

※ YOU WIN BY MAKING GUYS FEEL LIKE
WINNERS!

☆ ☆ EVERY RELATIONSHIP COUNTS!!!
☆ A TEENAGER WENT DOWN TO THE CANDY STORE TO BUY
SOME CANDY FOR HIS FIRST DATE. HE TOLD THE CANDY STORE OWNER
THAT HE WANTED TO BUY THREE BOXES OF CANDY:

ONE $5 BOX IF SHE SMILES AT ME AND ACTS LIKE SHE
LIKES ME.

A $10 BOX IF SHE WANTS TO HOLD HANDS
AND

A $15 BOX IF SHE WANTS TO KISS!

THE NIGHT OF THE DATE HE SHOWS UP AT HIS GIRL'S HOUSE, HE
KNOCKS ON THE DOOR AND HER DAD ANSWERS. HER DAD SAYS,
"HEY YOU'RE A LITTLE EARLY, BUT SINCE YOU'RE HERE YOU CAN
HAVE DINNER WITH US. WOULD YOU MIND SAYING OUR TABLE
PRAYER?" HE PRAYED AND PRAYED, IT WENT ON FOR ABOUT 25
MINUTES, FINALLY HE SAID AMEN! THE GIRL LOOKED AT HER DATE
AND SAID "I DIDN'T KNOW YOU WERE SO RELIGIOUS!" HE LOOKED
BACK AND SAID "I DIDN'T KNOW YOUR DAD OWNED THE CANDY
STORE"!

RELATIONSHIPS!!! ANOTHER GREAT
PASTOR KEN STORY ☆

Mahatma Gandhi once said that there are 7 things that will socially destroy us if we're not careful. Ghandi said them, Stephen Covey made them more famous. I learned them from a Marine friend of mine.

Talk about prophetic!!!

1. WEALTH WITHOUT WORK

Basically, expecting something for doing nothing that sense of entitlement can be very destructive. Some athletes get that sense of entitlement. Some people get that sense of entitlement.

2. PLEASURE WITHOUT CONSCIENCE

We have a Pro-Noun Problem, what's in it for me?
What do I get out of the deal?
The "I" needs to change to "US"!!!

Radical changes in minute measures.
Earthquakes and hurricanes get the most publicity,
but termites do the most damage.

Research shows we're going to be dead a lot longer
then we're alive, so let's make sure that we
LIVE RIGHT!

3. KNOWLEDGE WITHOUT CHARACTER

What's more dangerous? A little bit of knowledge with no character, or a lot of knowledge with no character?

Paul The Apostle Paul wrote to the Galatians about character 2000 years ago, he called it the FRUITS OF THE SPIRIT:

Love, Joy, Peace, Patience, Kindness, Goodness, Faith, Gentleness and Self Control. GAL. 5:22

Think we could teach that?

Anne Frank, a World War II victim, said this one time when talking about her life.

"My life — my personality, my habits, even my speech is a combination of the books I choose to read, the people I choose to listen to and the thoughts I choose to tolerate in my mind. Before the war, when I was a little girl, my Papa took me to the park on a Saturday afternoon to hear the orchestra play. At the end of the concert, from behind the musicians, a hundred helium balloons of red, yellow, blue and green floated up into the sky. It was so wonderful. I tugged on my Papa's arm and asked, "Papa, which color balloon will go the highest?" He said to me, "Anne, it's not the color of the balloon that is important. It's what's inside that makes all the difference." Anne added this, "I don't believe that being Jewish or Aryan or African has any bearing on what one can become. Greatness does not care if one is a girl or a boy. If, in fact, it is what's inside us that makes all the difference, then the difference is made when we choose what goes inside."

Pretty much nails it!

4. Business without Ethics

Understand that God did not put in me the ability to always make the right decisions. He did, however, put in me the ability to make a decision and then make it right!

5. SCIENCE WITHOUT HUMANITY

THERE ARE SOME LEADERS THAT DON'T GET THIS PRINCIPLE
AND ARE PUSHING US TOWARDS DESTRUCTION.

6. RELIGION WITHOUT SACRIFICE

ARE YOU A SPECTATOR OR ARE YOU A PARTICIPATOR? ARE
YOU A FOLLOWER OR YOU A LEADER? IT TAKES A LITTLE
SACRIFICE TO FOLLOW, BUT IT TAKES MUCH MORE TO
LEAD THE CHARGE.

7. POLITICS WITHOUT PRINCIPLE

ALL OF US COULD WRITE A BOOK ABOUT THIS, BUT I'M
NOT GOING TO. POLITICS WITHOUT PRINCIPLE PRETTY
MUCH SAYS IT ALL.

* SO WHERE DOES ALL THIS FIT WITH ME AND LEADING A TEAM.
AS THE LEADER, I DEAL WITH ALL 7 IDEALS, WEALTH, PLEA-
SURE, KNOWLEDGE, BUSINESS, SCIENCE, RELIGION
AND POLITICS. EVERY ONE OF THOSE TOPICS ARE A BASIS FOR
DAILY OPERATION.

IN PRO FOOTBALL, MORE SO THAN ON OTHER LEVELS OF FOOT-
BALL THAT I'VE WORKED, I CAN SAY THIS.
AS FOR:

WEALTH: THE PLAYERS PLAY FOR MONEY, THAT'S THEIR JOB.
SOME THINK THEY'RE WORTH MORE THAN THEY'RE GETTING PAID AND
SOME ARE GETTING PAID MORE THAN WHAT THEY'RE WORTH!

PLEASURE: THE GAME OF FOOTBALL IS FUN, BUT THE BUSINESS OF FOOTBALL, ON THE OTHER HAND, IS NOT ALWAYS SO MUCH FUN. WITH ALL THE BIG CONTRACTS AND MONEY INVOLVED, IT OFTEN GETS TO BE A PRO-NOUN PROBLEM, YOU KNOW THE "I — ME — MY" PROBLEM.

KNOWLEDGE: SOME GUYS KNOW A LOT, SOME GUYS THINK THEY KNOW A LOT. SOME GUYS HAVE GOOD CHARACTER, SOME GUYS THINK THEY HAVE GOOD CHARACTER. ALL IN ALL, THE GUYS THAT LACK KNOWLEDGE AND LACK CHARACTER RARELY LAST IN ANY BUSINESS, THERE ARE ALWAYS EXCEPTIONS, BUT NOT MANY!

BUSINESS: I'VE NEVER WORKED ON WALL STREET, BUT I CAN'T THINK OF A MORE COMPETITIVE BUSINESS ENVIRONMENT THAN THE NFL. THERE ARE FEW GUARANTEES ON ANYTHING. THERE IS ONE GUARANTEE THOUGH, IF YOU DON'T COMPETE YOU WILL LOSE YOUR JOB! THERE ARE ONLY ABOUT 96 QUARTERBACKS IN THE NFL AND THE ONES THAT HAVE THE JOB ARE NOT WILLING TO GIVE IT UP THAT EASY. COMPETE OR BE REPLACED! IT'S THE LAW OF THE JUNGLE. THE STRONG SURVIVE!

SCIENCE: JUST THINK ABOUT STEROIDS AND HUMAN GROWTH HORMONES. THE HOURS AND HOURS OF CONDITIONING AND WEIGHT TRAINING. ALL THAT STUFF. THAT'S JUST PART OF THE SCIENCE THAT GOES INTO IT. YOU GET THE REST OF THE PICTURE!

RELIGION: YOU'LL FIND OUT REAL QUICK WHERE YOUR FAITH IS WHEN YOU GET TESTED! EVERY DAY IS A TEST, EVERY GAME IS ANOTHER TEST!

POLITICS: Have you ever walked into your boss's office and he gives you the "we're heading in a different direction" speech? Or maybe you're the boss that's given that talk. You ask why and he says "because we've decided to head in a different direction" Time to pack up your stuff and leave and chalk one up to POLITICS!

There may be more than 7 social sins, but I think Gandhi pretty much hit the nail on the head. I don't think he ever coached a team or worked on Wall Street, but he got it!!!

Coach Sam Rutigiano told me this once:
We as coaches need to do this —
MASTER THESE THREE A's
ASSESS the TALENT
ACCUMULATE more TALENT
AND
ADJUST the TALENT

IT'S COACHING!!!
NC STATES STAFF ROOM

The tongue is the only tool that gets sharper with use!

LEADERSHIP TRAITS

MARINES LOOK FOR THESE CHARACTERISTICS WHEN LOOKING FOR THE NEXT LEADER

* **JUDGEMENT** – CAN HE ASSES AND JUDGE THE OUTCOME?

* **JUSTICE** – WHEN IT COMES TO STRESSFUL SITUATIONS IS HE AN EVEN KEEL PREDICTABLE MAN?

* **DEPENDABILITY** – DOES HE HAVE A CONSISTENT PERSONALITY?

* **INITIATIVE** – CAN HE TAKE ACTION WITHIN THE ABSENCE OF DIRECTIONS?

* **DECISIVENESS** – DOES HE HAVE THE ABILITY TO MAKE SOUND, ACCURATE AND TIMELY DECISIONS? GUYS, IN THE BATTLE, WILL FOLLOW THE MAN WHO GIVES THEM THE MOST CONFIDENCE, THE PLAN THAT WILL SAVE THEIR LIFE.

GENERAL GEORGE PATTON ONCE TOLD HIS TROOPS "I DON'T WANT ANY COMMUNIQUES SAYING YOU ARE HOLDING YOUR POSITION. WE'RE NOT HOLDING ANYTHING. WE'LL LET THE ENEMY TRY TO DO THAT. WE'RE ATTACKING DAY AND NIGHT!"

* **INTEGRITY** – DOES HE HAVE PERFECT VALOR? WILL HE BEHAVE WITHOUT WITNESS AS IF THE WHOLE WORLD WERE WATCHING?

ABRAHAM LINCOLN WAS ASKED WHETHER HE THOUGHT THAT GOD WAS ON HIS SIDE. HIS RESPONSE WAS SOMETHING LIKE THIS:
"DO I BELIEVE THAT GOD IS ON MY SIDE? TO BE HONEST, I HAVEN'T GIVEN THAT QUESTION VERY MUCH ATTENTION. I AM MUCH MORE CONCERNED WITH WHETHER WE ARE ON GOD'S SIDE!"

* <u>ENTHUSIASM</u> - IS HE FILLED WITH LEGITIMATE ENERGY
FOR THE TASK? SOME PEOPLE HAVE IT FOR
35 SECONDS, SOME HAVE IT FOR 35 YEARS!!!

* <u>BEARING</u> - HOW YOU LOOK AND CARRY YOURSELF, HOW YOU
ACT AND WHO YOU ARE!

A "REAL PRO QB" CARRIES HIMSELF DIFFERENTLY, AND EVERYONE
ON THE TEAM KNOWS HE'S THE QB.

OUR VERY LIVES ARE FASHIONED BY OUR CHOICES.
FIRST WE MAKE CHOICES.
THEN OUR CHOICES MAKE US!

* <u>UNSELFISHNESS</u> - DOES HE UNDERSTAND THAT IT'S NOT
ABOUT HIM AND IT'S ALL ABOUT THE
TEAM?

WHAT MAKES A MARINE RUN FROM COVER? WHAT MAKES
HIM RUN OUT IN THE MIDDLE OF THE STREET TO SAVE A FALLEN
SOLDIER? MEN DON'T RUN FROM COVER FOR FEAR, IF ANYTHING
THEY RUN FOR COVER. FEAR WOULD KEEP THEM IN THEIR FOX
HOLE. MEN RUN FROM COVER FOR LOVE. THEY RUN FOR THE LOVE
OF OTHERS. THEY WILL DO WHATEVER IT TAKES TO GET AND KEEP
THERE MEN SAFE. LOVE IS WHAT BINDS THEM TOGETHER, NOT FEAR,
PURE SELFLESSNESS!!!

* <u>COURAGE</u> - DOES HE HAVE THE COURAGE AND ABILITY TO
STAND STRONG IN ALL THAT HE DOES AND SAYS?

THE ONLY WAY TO AVOID CRITICISM IS TO
DO NOTHING AND BE NOTHING!

* <u>KNOWLEDGE</u> — IS HE AN INTELLIGENT MAN?

        FOLLOWERS RESPOND TO SMART LEADERS

        IF YOU ARE DETERMINED TO WIN,
    YOU WILL HAVE TO SURROUND YOURSELF WITH WINNERS!

* <u>LOYALTY</u> — IS HE LOYAL TO THE TEAM? IS HE LOYAL TO
        THE MISSION?

* <u>ENDURANCE</u> — CAN HE MENTALLY, PHYSICALLY, AND
        SPIRITUALLY HANDLE WHAT IS ABOUT TO HAPPEN?
        WE'RE GOING TO MARCH ON REGARDLESS IF WE'RE
        HEALTHY OR NOT. LET'S DO IT HEALTHY, <u>MENTALLY,</u>
        <u>PHYSICALLY</u> AND <u>SPIRITUALLY.</u>

          <u>WE DON'T QUIT!!!</u>

    MOST PEOPLE FAIL AT WHATEVER THEY ATTEMPT BECAUSE
OF AN UNDECIDED HEART.
    SHOULD I? SHOULD I NOT? GO FORWARD? GO BACK?
SUCCESS REQUIRES THE EMOTIONAL BALANCE OF A COMMIT-
TED HEART. WHEN CONFRONTED WITH A CHALLENGE, THE COMMITTED
HEART WILL SEARCH FOR A SOLUTION. THE UNDECIDED HEART WILL
SEARCH FOR AN ESCAPE!
    YOU DON'T REALLY BEGIN TO TRAIN UNTIL YOU GO AS FAR
AS YOU THINK YOU CAN GO AND THEN FORCE YOURSELF TO GO
ANOTHER STEP.

WE DON'T QUIT!!!

PAIN IS TEMPORARY. IT MAY LAST A MINUTE, OR AN HOUR, OR A DAY, OR A YEAR, BUT EVENTUALLY IT WILL SUBSIDE AND SOMETHING ELSE WILL TAKE IT'S PLACE. IF I QUIT, HOWEVER, IT LASTS FOREVER. SO WHEN I FEEL LIKE QUITTING I ASK MYSELF, WHICH WOULD I RATHER LIVE WITH?

— LANCE ARMSTRONG —

THERE'S A POINT IN EVERY RACE WHEN A RIDER ENCOUNTERS HIS REAL OPPONENT AND UNDERSTANDS THAT ITS HIMSELF.

THAT'S IT! ☆

COACH HOLTZ

OPPORTUNITY'S NOT NICE! IT WON'T WAIT AROUND FOR YOU TO TAKE ADVANTAGE OF IT!

COACH HOLTZ USED TO SAY TO OUR TEAM ON SATURDAYS BEFORE WE LEFT OUR LOCKER ROOM:

"FELLAS, WE DON'T HAVE TO BE THE BEST TEAM IN AMERICA TODAY, WE JUST HAVE TO BE THE BEST TEAM ON THIS FIELD, IN THIS GAME, THE REST WILL TAKE CARE OF ITSELF.

I ALWAYS LOVED THIS QUOTE EVER SINCE I COACHED AT NEVADA WITH CHRIS AULT

THE STRENGTH OF THE WOLF IS THE PACK AND THE STRENGTH OF THE PACK IS THE WOLF!!!

RUDYARD KIPLING

WE WERE THE WOLFPACK AND EVERY PLAYER ON THE TEAM KNEW THIS QUOTE, THIS WAS OUR IDENTITY AND WHO WE PLAYED FOR AND HOW WE PLAYED WAS ALL BASED ON THIS SAYING

WE ARE HUMAN BEINGS, NOT HUMAN DOINGS. MOST OF US GET CONFUSED AND THINK WE'RE HUMAN DOINGS.
IF WHO WE ARE IS WHAT WE DO,
THEN WHO ARE WE WHEN WE NO LONGER DO WHAT WE DO?

IT IS TRUE
THAT AN ARMY OF SHEEP LED BY A LION
WOULD DEFEAT
AN ARMY OF LIONS LED BY A SHEEP?

I LOVE THIS!!!

A GREAT WAY TO GET WHAT YOU WANT IS TO BREAK THE EVENT DOWN TO THE FUNDAMENTALS OF WHAT IT TAKES TO GET WHAT YOU WANT. KNOW WHAT THE PICTURE IS SUPPOSED TO LOOK LIKE IN THE END AND WORK TOWARD THAT GOAL. PARTICULARLY IN HIGH PRESSURE, INTENSE, CRITICAL SITUATIONS, THE DISCIPLINED TEAM, WHETHER IT'S FOOTBALL, FIREMEN OR NAVY SEALS ARE NOT GOING TO MAKE MISTAKES. AND THE REASON IS, THEY'VE PRACTICED IT A THOUSAND TIMES!

CREATE CONFIDENCE!!!   MAKE 'EM LOVE IT

I REMEMBER WHEN I WAS AT NOTRE DAME AND WE WERE PRACTICING TO BEAT OUR HUGE RIVAL MICHIGAN, AT MICHIGAN, COACH HOLTZ BROUGHT TONY RICE, OUR QB, UP IN FRONT OF OUR TEAM AND TOLD HIM, "HEY TONY, I TALKED TO BO TODAY" (BO SCHEMBECHLER, MICHIGAN'S HEAD COACH) "OH YEAH COACH, WHAT'D HE SAY?" TONY ASKED. COACH HOLTZ SAID, "HE TOLD ME THAT THE WOLVERINES WERE GOING TO PRACTICE TWICE TODAY, WHAT DO YOU

THINK OF THAT?" TONY SAID, "THAT'S NOT GOOD ENOUGH IF THEY WANT TO BEAT US COACH! "WHY'S THAT? ASKED COACH. "'CAUSE YOU KNOW WE'RE GONNA PRACTICE THREE TIMES AND WE'RE GONNA BE OUT HERE ALL NIGHT!" EVERYONE LAUGHED, BECAUSE WE WERE GOING TO PRACTICE AT LEAST THREE TIMES THAT DAY NO MATTER WHAT, EVEN IF IT TOOK <u>ALL</u> <u>NIGHT!</u>

BUT GUESS WHO WON THAT GAME? THE FIGHTING IRISH. WE WENT IN KNOWING WE WERE PREPARED AND CONFIDENT TO TAKE ON WHATEVER WAS COMING AT US.

<u>DISCIPLINE</u> – MEN WANT DISCIPLINE. DEEP DOWN THEY DESIRE ROUTINE. THEY SECRETLY WANT STRICT LIMITS. THEY WANT TO BE SHARP AND THEY WANT TO FEEL LIKE THEY'RE SPECIAL.

"GREAT PLAYERS AND GREAT TEAMS WANT TO BE DRIVEN! AVERAGE PLAYERS AND AVERAGE TEAMS WANT IT EASY!"
OKLAHOMA'S TEAM ROOM

<u>STANDARDS</u> – WE'LL ALWAYS PLAY AGAINST OUR HIGHEST STANDARD, NOT OUR OPPONENT'S.

IGNORE THE CRITICS – "IF YOU'RE WINNING YOU DON'T NEED THEM AND IF YOU'RE LOSING THEY CAN'T HELP YOU."
FRITZ CHRISLER
"WHAT DOES IT TAKE TO IGNORE THE CRITICS? IT TAKES ONE THING: CONFIDENCE. WHERE DO YOU GET CONFIDENCE? THROUGH PREPARATION!!!

GREAT TEAMS ARE DEFINED BY

PRACTICE HABITS – EVERY TEAM WANTS TO WIN, NOT EVERY TEAM HAS THE WILL TO PREPARE TO WIN.

HABITS
TOUGHNESS
CONFIDENCE
CONSISTENCY
VISION
CHEMISTRY

→ NO EXCUSES!
WE EXPECT TO WIN!
WE PREPARE TO WIN!
AND
WE WILL WIN!!!
BOB STOOPS HC OKLAHOMA

I WILL PREPARE MYSELF AND WHEN THE TIME COMES,
I WILL BE READY!
— ABRAHAM LINCOLN —

WE ARE WHAT WE REPEATEDLY DO.
EXCELLENCE, THEREFORE, IS A HABIT.
— ARISTOTLE —

MENTAL TOUGHNESS – YOU CAN EASILY DETERMINE THE CALIBER OF A PERSON BY THE AMOUNT OF OPPOSITION IT TAKES TO DISCOURAGE HIM.

MOST PEOPLE RACE TO SEE WHO IS THE FASTEST.
I RACE TO SEE WHO HAS THE MOST GUTS!
STEVE PREFONTAINE
IN THE NIKE SHOP IN EUGENE

Through my illness I learned rejection. I was written off.
That was the moment I thought, Okay, game on.
No prisoners. Everybody's going down.
— Lance Armstrong —

<u>CONFIDENCE</u> — You can judge the size of a person
by the size of the problem he is willing to face.

There's a direct correlation between a team that has no self-
esteem and it's weight program!
Bob Stoops — Oklahoma

<u>CONSISTENCY</u> — If you're not good all the time, you're
not good! _Bo—

<u>VISION</u> — Fundamentals Win —
The 7 principles to winning the game
1. Relentless Attack —
2. Out Hit your Opponent —
3. Make big plays —
4. Win the Turn over Battle —
5. Win the Special Teams Battle—
6. Eliminate Penalties —
7. Win on the Goal Line and Short Yardage —

Lou

I learned these principles way back when I was coaching at Notre Dame. We had a plan and we chalked it, we
talked it and we walked it all the time!

When I became the Head Coach at Wartburg, I added to the basic 7 and made it fit my style. I called it the "Big 7", and talked about Never Flinching. Every guy on the team memorized "The Big 7". They knew that was our plan and that was how we were going to play. We were graded as a team and as individuals within these areas. Our plan broke it down to the situational fundamentals of the game. When we achieved these goals we had a great chance of winning.

"THE BIG 7"

— Fundamentals Win —

1. Relentless Attack —
2. Out Hit your Opponent —
3. Make Big plays — Big plays happen when all eleven of us do the right thing
4. Win the Turn over Battle —
5. Win the Special Teams Battle — Hidden yardage
6. Eliminate Penalties —
7. Win on the Goal Line and Short Yardage —

— NEVER FLINCH —

We had all the confidence in the world, knowing that our plan worked. We never flinched. We ran a relentless attack in all three phases of the game and our players bought into the plan and believed.

Football games are no different than any other competition. Have a vision, prepare a plan, work your plan, and grade everything according to the plan. Evaluate what went on and then you have a standard from which to judge your talent base, your direction, and your achievements.

<u>CHEMISTRY</u> – Every practice, every game, every player and every coach changes the chemistry of our team. It's like water, when you add something to water, it's no longer water, it's coffee, it's Kool-Aid, or beer it's not just water anymore. Good or bad, it's changed. Just like how water changes when you add something to it, teams change when you add something to them, competition, practice, games, whatever it is, the team never stays the same.

To be or not to be...
That is not the question.
How to be or How not to be.
That's the real question!!!

FAST, PHYSICAL,
FUNDAMENTAL FOOTBALL PLAYER
THAT DOES WHATEVER IT TAKES TO WIN
THAT LEAVES NO DOUBT!

This was our mantra at Fresno State. This was who we were. Every game we wanted to be the fastest, most physical, fundamental team on the field. We wanted to play harder than our opponent, so hard that it showed!

I added SMART to the front of this statement, and use it with my group to this day. There's nothing better on the football field than a SMART player that possesses all these skills.

MAKE IT
HAPPEN!

SMART, FAST, PHYSICAL,
FUNDAMENTAL FOOTBALL PLAYER
THAT DOES WHATEVER IT TAKES TO WIN
AND LEAVES NO DOUBT!

– OPPORTUNITY –

DURING ONE OF OUR TEAM MEETINGS, WE TOOK A FOOTBALL AND USED IT AS A TOOL. WE ASKED A QUESTION AND RANDOMLY TOSSED THE BALL AROUND TO DIFFERENT PLAYERS. WHOEVER CAUGHT THE BALL HAD TO PLAY, HAD TO SPEAK UP. YOU WEREN'T ALLOWED TO SAY "I DON'T KNOW" OR "I DON'T CARE". YOU HAD TO HAVE AN OPINION AND YOU HAD TO SAY IT. EVERYONE IN THE ROOM WAS INCLUDED, COACHES, PLAYERS, EVERYONE.

QUESTIONS LIKE; WHAT'S IT GOING TO TAKE TO CHANGE OUR TEAM? WHAT ARE YOU GOING TO DO TO CHANGE IT? THE BALL GOT TOSSED, FROM COACH TO PLAYER, PLAYER TO COACH, EVERYONE HAD A SHOT AT IT. THE BALL REPRESENTS OPPORTUNITY. WHEN OPPORTUNITY COMES YOUR WAY YOU NEED TO TAKE ADVANTAGE OF IT AND MAKE THE BEST OF IT. YOU NEVER KNOW WHEN OPPORTUNITY IS GOING TO COME YOUR WAY, YOU NEED TO EXPECT IT AND BE PREPARED WHEN IT COMES. DO YOU WANT THE BALL WHEN THE GAME IS ON THE LINE? OR SO YOU PANIC AND CHOKE WHEN THE BALL COMES YOUR WAY?

WE WANT YOU
WHEN YOU'RE READY TO WIN A CHAMPIONSHIP!
OHIO STATES STAFF ROOM

We had a team meeting where we asked the guys to list which qualities in a player will it take to win a championship. Qualities, which combined, result in high character like trustworthiness, integrity, honesty, reliability, loyalty and accountability. These were just some of the traits that were yelled out. There were 18 traits listed before anyone yelled out talent.

Talent is definitely part of winning a championship, a big part, but so is character and all the things that it comprises. A talented player that lacks character will not succeed like the player that possesses it all. Most of all we didn't want any of our guys to think they weren't talented enough to win, nor did we want them to make excuses comparing themselves to the other teams.

Character is about black and white! When you search for the grey areas you weaken your character
Pat Tillman

When you throw mud,
you have less ground to stand on.

David didn't see Goliath as bigger than him,
he saw Goliath as smaller than God!!
1 Samuel 17

Do we cut?

Not everyone can be on the team. That's probably one of the hardest realizations of a leader, that not everyone can be on the team. As a leader you want to see that everyone has a place and or that you can save every player

I'VE HAD LOTS OF GUYS COME INTO MY OFFICE AND CALL IT QUITS, FOR MANY DIFFERENT REASONS. I LEARNED A LONG TIME AGO THAT I NEED TO LISTEN, BUT I DON'T NEED TO TRY TO CONVINCE THEM TO STAY. THAT SOUNDS COLD BUT, BY THE TIME THEY SHOW UP IN MY OFFICE THEIR MIND IS MADE UP. I'VE CONVINCED SOME TO STAY, ONLY TO HAVE THE SAME CONVERSATION A WHILE LATER I'VE FOUND IT BEST TO LET THEM FIGURE OUT WHERE THEIR COMMITMENT IS AND DECIDE WHAT TO DO ON THEIR OWN. I'VE LEARNED THIS ABOUT BEING PART OF A TEAM.

WHO'S GOING TO SACRIFICE? — SOME GUYS WON'T

CHANGE. THEY KNOW THEIR COMFORT ZONES AND DON'T WANT TO LEAVE IT. THEY WON'T PUSH THEMSELVES BEYOND THEIR COMFORT ZONE. THEY CAN BE KNOWN AS A "CANCER" THEIR ATTITUDE IS A KILLER AND DIVIDES THE TEAM.

WHO'S GOING TO COMPETE? — SOME GUYS AREN'T UP TO

THE CHALLENGE. THERE ARE DIFFERENT LEVELS OF COMPETITION. SOME DON'T REALLY UNDERSTAND THE AMOUNT OF COMMITMENT IT TAKES TO BE THE BEST.

— COMPETE —

RUNNING A FOOTBALL TEAM IS NO DIFFERENT FROM RUNNING ANY OTHER KIND OF ORGANIZATION, AN ARMY, A BUSINESS, IT'S ALL ONE IN THE SAME. THE PRINCIPLES ARE THE SAME, THE OBJECTIVE IS TO WIN, TO BEAT THE OTHER GUY.

IT IS THE REALITY OF LIFE THAT MEN ARE COMPETITIVE AND THE MOST COMPETITIVE GAMES DRAW THE MOST COMPETITIVE MEN. THAT'S WHY THEY'RE THERE, TO COMPETE! THEY KNOW THE RULES AND THE OBJECTIVES WHEN THEY GET IN THE GAME. THE OBJECTIVE IS TO WIN — FAIRLY, SQUARELY, DECENTLY, BY THE RULES, BUT WIN!

AND IN TRUTH, I'VE NEVER KNOWN A MAN WORTH HIS SALT

WHO IN THE LONG RUN, DEEP DOWN IN HIS HEART, DIDN'T APPRECI-
ATE THE GRIND, THE DISCIPLINE. THERE IS SOMETHING IN GOOD MEN
THAT REALLY YEARNS FOR THE DISCIPLINE AND THE HARSH REALITY OF
HEAD-TO-HEAD COMBAT.

 I DON'T SAY THESE THINGS BECAUSE I BELIEVE IN THE BRUTE
NATURE OF MAN OR THAT MEN MUST BE BRUTALIZED TO BE COM-
BATIVE. I BELIEVE IN GOD, AND I BELIEVE IN HUMAN DECENCY. BUT I
FIRMLY BELIEVE THAT ANY MAN'S FINEST HOUR — HIS GREATEST FUL-
FILLMENT TO ALL HE HOLDS DEAR — IS THAT MOMENT WHEN HE HAS
WORKED HIS HEART OUT IN A GOOD CAUSE AND LIES EXHAUSTED ON
THE FIELD OF BATTLE — VICTORIOUS!!!
    — VINCE LOMBARDI —

  YOU'RE ONLY A VICTIM ONCE,
  AFTER THAT YOU'RE A VOLUNTEER
   NAOMI JUDD

WHO HAS THE ABILITY? — SOME GUYS ARE JUST BET-
TER PLAYERS THAN OTHERS, FOR WHAT EVER REASONS, SOME "GET
IT" MORE THAN OTHERS. I CAN PLAY FOOTBALL BETTER THAN I CAN
PLAY THE GUITAR. I CAN PRACTICE THE GUITAR ALL DAY AND STILL
MIGHT NOT BE AS GOOD AS THE GUY WHO "GET'S IT"!!!

HERE'S SOME SIMPLE MATH:
   THE PLAYER THAT:
"GETS IT" — SACRIFICES — COMPETES = SENSE OF ENTITLEMENT
 SACRIFICES + COMPETES — "GETS IT" = TEAM PLAYER
 "GETS IT" + SACRIFICES + COMPETES = BIG TIME PLAYER

DO WE CUT? NO, WE DON'T HAVE TO BECAUSE MORE OFTEN THAN
NOT, EACH PLAYER DEFINES HIS ROLE THROUGH HIS CHARACTER AND

THE STANDARDS THAT ARE SET. WILL HIS CHARACTER LET HIS ABIL-
ITY COME THROUGH AND ALLOW HIM TO RISE TO THE CHALLENGE?
THAT'S ANOTHER QUESTION. SOMETIMES YES, SOMETIMES NO. SOME-
TIMES COMPETITION CRUSHES A PLAYER, SOMETIMES IT CATAPULTS
HIM TO ANOTHER LEVEL. WHAT'S INSIDE DETERMINES HOW HIGH HE'LL
RISE!!! ALL ROLES ARE DEFINED FOR THE GREATER GOOD OF THE
TEAM.

WHO'S GOING TO BE PART OF THE TEAM?

ONE IS TOO SMALL OF A NUMBER TO
ACHIEVE GREATNESS!!!

LANCE ARMSTRONG SAID IT BEST
"NO ONE ASCENDS ALONE!"

BEHIND AN ABLE MAN
THERE ARE ALWAYS OTHER ABLE MEN!
— CHINESE PROVERB —

EVALUATING THE TALENT

WHEN I WAS COACHING AT NOTRE DAME WE HAD AN EVALUATION
SYSTEM THAT EVERY PLAYER WAS SUBJECT TO, WE HAD EVERY GUY
FILL OUT THE FORM. BASICALLY IT WAS A SELF EVALUATION QUES-
TIONNAIRE THAT ASSESSED EVERYTHING FROM ACADEMICS TO TALENT
LEVEL. WE WANTED TO KNOW WHAT THEY THOUGHT OF THEMSELVES.
WE ALSO USED THIS AS A TALKING BASIS FOR TELLING THE PLAYER
WHERE HE WAS ON THE TEAM AND WHAT HE NEEDED TO DO TO BE
THE BEST TEAM PLAYER.

WE HAD 10 QUESTIONS WITH A SCALE FROM ONE TO TEN
THAT EACH PLAYER COULD PUT A NUMBER ON.

For instance, rate yourself from 1 to ten, ten being the best.

Right now are you an:

All-American	(10)
Starter on a Championship Team	(9)
Second Teamer	(8)
Role Player	(7)
Start on the Scout Team	(6)
Working hard	(5)
On the Team	(4)

Another question was,

What is your GPA right now?

4.0	(10)
3.5+	(9)
3.25+	(8)
3.0+	(7)
2.85+	(6)
2.75+	(5)
2.5+	(4)
2.49 –	(3)

So after we add up the scores, (maximum of 100 points) the player knows where he sits with himself and on the team. We as coaches would say that we needed to average an 85 or better as a team, for us to have a chance to play for the National Championship. If the players score added up to less or more than 85, then we all knew, players included, where we stood. It was a great tool which allowed us to keep a standard and have the players reach the standard.

We didn't have to cut because each player knew his Commitment level, His Ability, his willingness to be part of the team, and his level of competitiveness. All this was revealed through this process, this tool helped us make a championship quality team.

It's Not About The Bike

I learned what it means to ride the Tour de France. It's not about the bike. The race is a metaphor for life. It's not only the longest race in the world, but also the most exalting, heartbreaking, and potentially tragic. It poses every conceivable element to the rider, and more: cold, heat, mountains, plains, ruts, flat tires, winds, unspeakably bad luck, unthinkable beauty, yawning senselessness, and above all great, deep self-questioning. During our lives we're faced with so many different elements as well, we experience so many setbacks, and fight such hand-to-hand battles with failure, head down in the rain, just trying to stay upright and to have a little hope. The Tour is not just a bike race, not at all. It is a test. It tests you physically, it test you mentally, morally, and it even test you spiritually. There were no shortcuts, I realized. It took years of racing to build up the mind and body and character, until a rider had logged hundreds of races and thousands of miles of road. I wouldn't be able to win a Tour de France until I had enough iron in my legs, lungs, brain, and heart. I could not win until I was a man.

Lance Armstrong – It's Not About The Bike

It's never about the bike,
it's about who's on the bike!

Tim Tebow said this to the press after a loss to Ole Miss his junior year. He went on to lead his team to a National Championship that season.

"

To the fans and everybody in Gator Nation, I'm sorry. I'm extremely sorry. We were hoping for an undefeated season. That was my goal, something Florida has never done here. I promise you one thing, a lot of good will come out of this. You will never see any player in the entire country play as hard as I will play the rest of the season. You will never see someone push the rest of the team as hard as I will push everybody the rest of the season."

"You will never see a team play harder than we will the rest of the season."

"God Bless."

NEVER 7 FLINCH

I Can Do All Things Through Christ!

That's what I'm talkin' 'bout!!! Become accountable, take responsibility, and change what you can change, and NEVER FLINCH! Tim wasn't afraid to put it all out there and go after it! He knew what he wanted to do and how he wanted to do it. He changed his team by changing himself first. He raised the bar and lifted his team!!!

THE DIFFERENCE BETWEEN
THE ONE WHO MANAGES AND THE ONE WHO LEADS

A MANAGER:

* ADMINISTRATES ⟶ * INNOVATES

* MAINTAINS ⟶ * DEVELOPS

* ALL ABOUT SYSTEMS AND ⟶ * ALL ABOUT HIS PEOPLE
  FLOW CHARTS   (HIS TEAM)

* RELIES ON CONTROL ⟶ * RELIES ON TRUST

* ACCEPTS REALITY ⟶ * INVESTIGATES REALITY

* WORRIES ABOUT HOW AND WHEN ⟶ * WORRIES ABOUT WHAT AND WHY

* HAS AN EYE ON THE BOTTOM LINE ⟶ * HAS AN EYE ON THE HORIZON

* IMITATES ⟶ * ORIGINATES AND INITIATES

* ACCEPTS THE STATUS QUO ⟶ * CHALLENGES THE STATUS QUO

* DOES THINGS RIGHT ⟶ * DOES THE RIGHT THING
  (EVEN WHEN THE RIGHT THING ISN'T THE
  EASIEST)

A LEADER:

WARREN BENNIS
I GOT THIS FROM A MARINE FRIEND

It's Not About the Basil

My wife, Amy, loves basil. She usually starts growing small plants in pots early in the spring, so she can maximize her basil bounty. She went down to the local nursery, and bought a couple small starter plants, brought them home, and replanted them into bigger pots. After a few days in the kitchen window, the basil started to droop and lean over the edge of the pot. It looked bad, real bad!

We live in Cleveland, Ohio, and unfortunately, sunshine is a rare event in April, and the outside nights are too cold for the fragile new plants. I said to Amy "That basil looks weak!" She replied, "Well it needs to get a lot stronger!" I said back, "Well its not going to get any stronger when it doesn't have the sun pulling it up!" She said, "You know, that's true! That's true with everything. None of us get any stronger without the sun pulling us up!" We both looked at each other and said, "That's it!" We both thought it at the same time. "None of us have a chance without the <u>SON</u> pulling us up!" Leaders lift. That's what Jesus does, he lifts us up! We all need the sun/SON!!!

SERVING IT UP!

COACH MIKAYLA LINEBAUGH IS ONE GREAT COACH!! HOW 'BOUT STARTING YOUR VOLLEYBALL SEASON OFF WITH A 34 — 0 RE-CORD? SHE'S ALL ABOUT EXCELLENCE IN ALL THAT HER GIRLS DO. HER RECIPE FOR SUCCESS GOES LIKE THIS;

ONE CUP DETERMINATION,

ONE CUP TEAM CHEMISTRY,

3 CUPS HARD WORK

AND

A DASH OF TALENT.

SHE GETS EVERYTHING OUT OF HER GIRLS AND THEN SOME. MIKAYLA HAS A GREAT PASSION FOR HER COACHING AND IT SHOWS IN EVERYTHING THAT SHE DOES. SHE'S ALL ABOUT "CHANGE THE GIRLS, CHANGE THE TEAM." SHE'S MAGICALLY CHANNELED THE 15 AND 16 YEAR OLD GIRLS HEARTS AWAY FROM TEXTING AND MYSPACING TO SHAR-ING AND CARING, NOT ONLY FOR THEIR TEAM MATES, BUT FOR THE TOWN WHERE THEY LIVE.

WINNING STARTS OFF THE COURT FOR HER TEAM. THE GAME IS BIGGER THAN THE VOLLEYBALL COURT, AND COACH LINEBAUGH GETS IT. SHE GET'S, "NEVER FLINCH," SHE GETS, "WE'RE ALL CONNECTED ALL THE TIME," AND SHE GETS, "OWNERSHIP EQUALS CHAMPIONSHIPS!!!" MOST OF ALL SHE GETS, "LEADERS LIFT," AND SHE LIVES IT! SHE HAS LIFTED HER GIRLS BEYOND THEIR WILDEST DREAMS! SHE ENDED THAT LAST SEASON 58 — 4. THIS YEAR COACH LINEBAUGH'S GIRLS WERE 55 — 8, THAT'S 113 — 12 FOR ALL YOU MATHEMATICIANS OUT THERE!!!

OH, I FORGOT TO MENTION, HER SOFTBALL TEAM IS 10 — 0 AS OF THIS WRITING. AND YOU THOUGHT SHE JUST COACHED GIRLS VOL-LEYBALL! LIKE HER GIRLS WOULD SAY, "WHATEVER!!!"

IT STARTS WITH US

Ultimately we're all leaders, parents, teachers, coaches, team mates, no one gets off the hook. The game of life is not played with shoulder pads and helmets, although it would be nice at times. Everyday we rely on each other for our protection and success, we're all connected all the time. We need a leader, because GOOD LEADERS LIFT! One of us inspires another one of us to do things we never dreamed of doing. WE ARE THE EXAMPLE!!!

I've been reading up on "CHI" lately. "CHI" is what the Chinese define as energy, that which gives life. To use a biblical reference, it is what God breathed into the dust to produce Adam. Just think, if at any time in your life, you could give someone their "CHI." If you could breathe some life into your Family, your Team, or your Friends, and show them how to be more than they ever thought they'd become!

WHAT IF YOU COULD LEAD THEM?
WHAT IF YOU COULD LIFT THEM?!?!?!

LaVergne, TN USA
11 February 2011
216250LV00001B/1/P